T0368497

DALEY QUOTES

Bringing out the best in you from the inside out

MARTWEZ DALEY

Xlibris
844-714-8691
www.Xlibris.com

ISBN: Softcover   978-1-6641-9584-4
        EBook   978-1-6641-9585-1

Rev. date: 11/20/2021

DALEY QUOTES

Bringing out the best in you from the inside out

INTRO SUMMARY

Hello my name is Martwez Daley. I was born December 21, 1977. That day God blessed me with life. One thing about life is that it's amazing. Once you understand that you will see. I've been through all of things in my life that could of shifted me in another direction. The fact of the matter is that your greatest gift you posed is your choices. Always choose to give yourself the best no matter what the situation or circumstances. See I realized that when you come from something great. You have to behave in the same manner as your creator in order to receive everything you desire. God thought process is not negative so yours shouldn't.

MIND

Talking about the mind is very delicate reason. Is that your conscious holds everything. So what happened was that the people that put this system in place. Knew exactly what they were doing. See they want to feed you negativity so the conscious could retain it and have you act out that behavior. When a certain situation presents itself. The saying is that if you over indulge in something it becomes a part of you. So the reason behind that is that they don't want you to become who you truly are. So they put you in a system that taught you to think backwards. That's how they have the control over you when they keep feeding you something over and over again. That's when hypnosis takes over your conscious and that's when you're doing things you know is wrong and agreeing with what's right negativity keeps you hypnotized. Positivity keeps you in your true state. I'm just asking you to give yourself what you deserve and that's only through positivity which starts in the mind.

Stop allowing a false representation of you to become you.

Determination brings your ability to its peak.

Being determined exposes your true ability.

The only way to see your fullest potential is by giving it your all at the moment.

The most important thing you have in this world
is your choices just never choose to doubt you.

A great attitude creates a great outcome.

Your hiding thoughts of you explains your success in life.

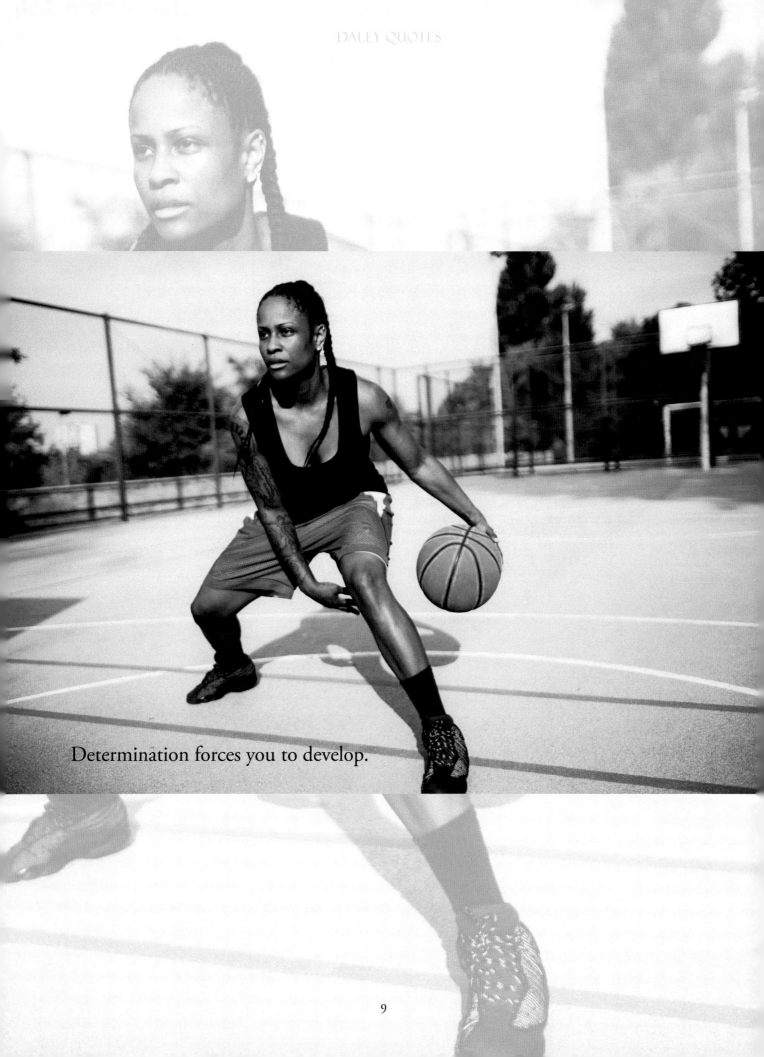

Determination forces you to develop.

Determination brings out what is already ordained in you.

Over talking creates lies.

Stop being afraid of what it takes to accomplish what you want.

I am forces you to be confident.

Your decisions exposes areas of growth and strength.

Stop being afraid of what you already know.

Your individual growth is in discipline.

Self-discipline creates you.

Truth eliminates people that mean you no good.

Writing your goals down shows you what you are supposed to be doing.

SPIRIT

The spiritual is something I am excited to talk about. See the spiritual version of you. Is the true you. Your outer shell which is your body is just there to protect you from things that is not true. The thing with your spirit is that it's only job is to keep you true to yourself. That's why when you're feeling uncomfortable on the inside. The true you is telling the false representation of you that you won't stand for it. See the thing about your spirit is that it's a pure replica of greatness. Its job is to make sure that you fulfill your true purpose while living. We have our own individual talents which makes us all unique in our own ways. We're supposed to come together and appreciate one another. For who we are see the spiritual you only wants the best for you the only way to achieve.

I am keeps you conscious of you.

Truth brings out all positivity in you.

Life explains itself in silence.

Your talents give you individuality.

Our truth has nothing to do with the truth.

The visions you see of you is the things you are destined to do.

A lot of us is searching for our true potential when we already know our potential.

Spiritually holds positivity and religion holds negativity.

I am is allowing us to experience life in the flesh.

The secret in controlling your life is to let go.

When you let go of you it's only then you will see you.

Hypnosis takes over when you obsessively indulge in negative thoughts.

Your why is your purpose.

Anything that is causing you in uncomfortable feeling
just look inside and it will always tell you your why.

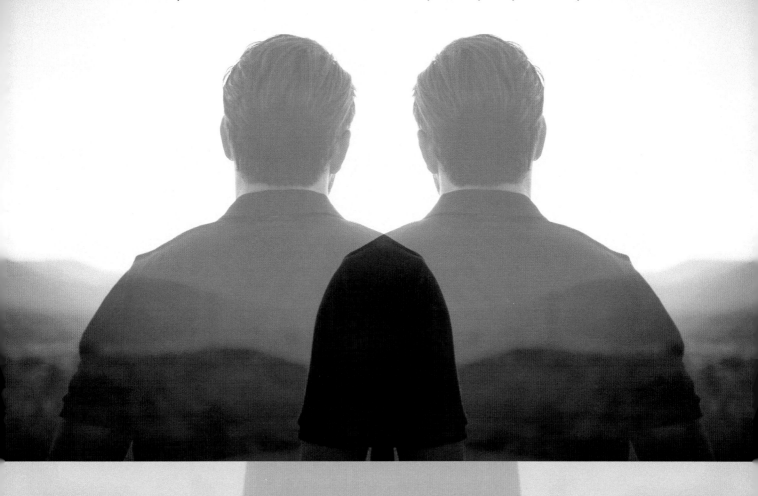

Only when you find peace within is when everything around you falls in place.

Retrain your brain from thinking insane thoughts about your true ability

You can accomplish anything you desire
with belief without a smitch of doubt.

Choose carefully the words you speak because your emotions are held accountable.

When you understand the meaning of silence
is only then you will understand you.

Step outside of you because it is never about you it's always about just development which is for you.

Being humble is a quiet place to find your true self.

Patience is experience
and experience is belief

The only reason fear appears is when you are afraid of finding your true self.

Always go for what's best for your inner peace.

You always want the best for you is just that
you only want what's best for you sometimes.

Your manual in life is within your true self.

When you keep making up excuses on
what you are doing you are not in your true self.

The only reason we complain is because we are not true to our decisions.

The unseen controls you if you don't know you

Unconditional is the universal language of your being.

Just knowing your why is everything else falls in place.

Based on your choices of thoughts explain the way you feel about you.

Knowing you is to not judge you.

Stop forming emotions off of what is.

Knowing you is to control you.

All your gifts lie on the other side of appreciation.

The moment keeps you living in your purpose.

Situation and circumstances
shouldn't dictate who you are.

Positivity is purpose.

Emotion clouds the actual factual.

Emotions forces scattered decisions.

Truth only represents good.

An idol mind is a uncomfortable spirit.

Printed in the United States
by Baker & Taylor Publisher Services